ACCUSATIONS

BELIEVING A LIE

DICK SORENSON

Compiled by
DONNA SORENSON AND TAMI GAUPP

Illustrated by
BECKY HANSEN

THE LANYAP LIFE BOOKS

Print ISBN: 9781736113981

eBook ISBN: 9798985927726

1116 Vista Avenue, #353, Boise, Idaho 83705

www.thelanyaplife.com

CONTENTS

HOW TO INTERACT WITH
THIS MATERIAL

Our suggestion to you, as you read this material, is that instead of trying to search your memory and recall events or incidents in your life that the topics in *Journey to Wholeness* could apply to, pray this simple prayer:

" Lord, I thank you that my life belongs to you. All the restoration that you plan to do in my life is in Your hands. Holy Spirit, I give You permission to bring any and all events and situations to my mind that You want to heal and restore.

As Psalm 23:3 says, "He restores my
soul; He guides me in the paths of
righteousness for His name's sake."

As He is leading, receive the restoration that happens as He helps you apply the principles in this series. Record the specifics of this restoration process. This will be your testimony of God's goodness and faithfulness to provide all of your needs. As He leads, you can share this testimony of God's miraculous provision with family and friends so God can use and bless it for generations.

Welcome fellow travelers on our journey to our inheritance as His sons and daughters!

Hiking toward hope on a personal journey to wholeness...

A message to you from Dick --

This series is called *Journey to Wholeness* because it is the journey the Lord is taking me on to become whole. I find it has changed me and will do the same for others. I would say, as you discover these truths, take time with the Lord and ask Him to give you revelation on how to apply these in your own life. This is great preparation for ministering to others and training others to minister.

May God guide and bless you as we journey together with Him. Welcome to The Journey!

—*DICK SORENSON*

CHAPTER 1
ACCUSATIONS

*W*hat are accusations?
The basic meaning of accusation in Hebrew means: "To devour, to lick, to chew up, to attack and conquer." The New Testament adds the meanings: "To crave, to question motive, violently cast down and scatter, to fatally kill with a weapon, and to unlawfully defraud."

In all of this, we see it's not in our best interest to be involved in judgments or accusations. Accusations and judgments are connected. All of us in this life have experienced both giving and receiving accusations and judgments.

Romans 8:1-2 states that we are not under accusations and condemning judgments in Christ Jesus. *Romans 8:31* says that God is for us and Christ Jesus died for us and intercedes for us.

Romans 8 verses 35-39 demonstrate how nothing

can separate us from the love of God. So, we will learn how to appropriate and live free from accusations and condemning judgments that Satan, the accuser, uses to defraud us of life. Let's continue our *Journey to Wholeness* as lies of accusations are exposed and truth is revealed.

As we live in this world, we are going to experience lies, accusations, and judgments. Why? Because, in the world, this is the way things happen.

People accuse each other.

- They accuse themselves
- They receive accusations
- They judge others
- They judge themselves

That is the world's system and the way it operates. Everything is supposed to fit into a particular culture and society, shaped and based on its values. So, you and I, living in the world, but not being of it, are going to experience the burdens and weight of accusations and judgments.

Even if we do the wrong thing and then we repent, there are still many times when the judgment or accusations may seem to cling to us and hang over us, waiting to steal and destroy.

Jesus understands that. He knew it and He experienced it while He was here on earth. Just look at His last day here on earth and the trials He went through. Look at all of the accusations which were hurled at Him and He experienced. But, as a result of that, He did not leave us alone here on earth. When He went back to heaven to sit at the right-hand of the Father, He sent a counselor, another advocate, a comforter: He sent the Holy Spirit, who would be with us leading us into the truth.

Read *John 14:16-18, and 26.*

God saw fit to provide us with everything we need for life and godliness. He is aware, as we walk and live in this life, that there are all kinds of dangers and problems we are unable to see. So, He gives us a guide to be with us. We have the Holy Spirit, when we accept Jesus Christ and are born again. We receive that life from the Father above. We are born and become a new creation with the Holy Spirit operating in us. Then, we are baptized in water into His death, burial, and resurrection. And we read in *1 John 5:6-8* the blood of Jesus was shed so that the Spirit, the water, and the blood, bear witness, as it says in *1 John 5*.

The new life we receive effects our spirit, our soul, and our body. The world we live in, the one the enemy has manipulated, affects our entire being. But the truth is; Christ is in us. And He is the hope of glory that overcomes the world and overcomes the effects of sin and the destruction it tries to bring.

CHAPTER 2
JESUS DOES NOT LEAVE US ALONE

*N*ow, let's look at the four points we need to remember when dealing with accusations.

1. Jesus sends us a counselor, a comforter.

- To be with us
- To lead us in the Truth

> *John 14:16-18, 26, "I will ask the*
> *Father, and He will give you*
> *another Helper, that He may be with*
> *you forever;* that is *the Spirit of*
> *truth, whom the world cannot*
> *receive, because it does not see Him*
> *or know Him,* but *you know Him*
> *because He abides with you and*

> *will be in you. I will not leave you*
> *as orphans; I will come to you."*
> *Verse 26, "But the Helper, the Holy*
> *Spirit, whom the Father will send in*
> *My name, He will teach you all*
> *things, and bring to your remem-*
> *brance all that I said to you."*

2. We have the Spirit, the water, and the blood; they bear witness.

> *1 John 5:4-12, "For whatever is born*
> *of God overcomes the world; and*
> *this is the victory that has overcome*
> *the world—our faith. Who is the one*
> *who overcomes the world, but he*
> *who believes that Jesus is the Son of*
> *God? This is the One who came by*
> *water and blood, Jesus Christ; not*
> *with the water only, but with the*
> *water and with the blood. It is the*
> *Spirit who testifies, because the*
> *Spirit is the truth. For there are*
> *three that testify: the Spirit and the*
> *water and the blood; and the three*
> *are in agreement. If we receive the*
> *testimony of men, the testimony of*
> *God is greater; for the testimony of*

*God is this, that He has testified
concerning His Son. The one who
believes in the Son of God has the
testimony in himself; the one who
does not believe God has made Him
a liar, because he has not believed
in the testimony that God has given
concerning His Son. And the testimony is this, that God has given us
eternal life, and this life is in His
Son. He who has the Son has the
life; he who does not have the Son
of God does not have the life."*

3. Accusations affect our spirit, soul, and body.

Accusations affect our spirit with a sense of heaviness
or cloudiness. Our soul is affected by constant negative
thoughts and our emotions of fear and anxiety grow.
The physiological responses of our body react nega-
tively in an automatic way.

4. God has made provision for us.

*In I John 2:1. John writes, "My little
children, I am writing these things
to you so that you may not sin. And
if anyone sins, we have an Advocate*

with the Father, Jesus Christ the righteous."

This is good news! He, Himself, is the payment for our sins. Not for ours only, but for those of the whole world. You may say, "But Jesus isn't here right now with me as I experience these accusations."

Jesus does not

leave us alone

Image 1 -We Do Not Have to Be Alone

But, in *John 14:16-18,* Jesus tells us that He isn't going to leave us alone. He said that when He leaves, He will send another comforter to us. This comforter will be with us. He will tell us what the truth is.

So, we have this other one, who is an Advocate with us, and He always leads us into what the truth is. You and I will be accused. Haven't we all experienced accusations? In this world, we will have problems, but Jesus said, *"Be encouraged, I have overcome the world."* (John 16:33)

CHAPTER 3
WHO INITIATES ACCUSATION?

*W*hen accusations come to our mind, we hear them internally, in our own voice. Thus, we assume that we are the one who is initiating these thoughts and accusations. We are completely unaware of how things really work.

Other times, we think it is God who is accusing us. Many times, other people are involved. It may be parents, friends, strangers, siblings, or some kind of enemy. We hear the accusations and judgments they make, and we assume that they are the source of those accusations.

We may listen to someone preach a sermon and our feelings tell us that their words are actually God coming after us: God condemning and judging us. We assume that either we are judging ourselves, that others are, or that God is judging us.

Ephesians 6:11 says that the battles and warfare we

are dealing with is not flesh and blood. But they look like flesh and blood: they look like people. That is how it looked when Jesus was on trial. All these people were screaming accusations at Him. Yet, He didn't answer them. He knew that those people were not the real problem, he knew they were not the real accusers.

In the same way, we need to understand who initiates accusations. Even though we are dealing with people, with flesh and blood, dealing with ourselves and our ideas about God, and what others have said: *it is not God*. God does not initiate accusations. We do not initiate accusations against ourselves. The one who does is Satan. He always accuses. He is called the accuser. He is the author of all accusations and deception. He was a liar from the beginning and he cannot tell the truth.

Revelation 12:10 says he is the accuser of the brethren and he accuses us before God day and night, he accuses us to our own mind, and he brings up accusations. He is also called the tempter. This is what temptation does; it accuses us.

Satan brings the accusations, presents them to us, and gets us to accept them. If we receive the temptation, if we swallow it, then we swallow the lie and we start living on the basis of that lie as though it were the truth. The deception then begins to steal from us and will begin to destroy what we have.

So how will Satan accuse us? The situations we face in life constantly change. Our enemy will often use that change as a point to bring accusations regarding the meaning of the change. He will tell us it's not good, that it is our fault, and others are out to get us. He knows how to manipulate our thoughts and feelings, causing us to blame others.

Satan uses any situation he can. He is the illegal god of this world. He isn't supposed to be, but because he is, he controls the world systems. He introduced them, and he is able to manipulate a conditioned response that will be destructive to us and others. He interprets circumstances you and I have lived through and experienced, telling us what he wants us to believe about those experiences even though it isn't the truth.

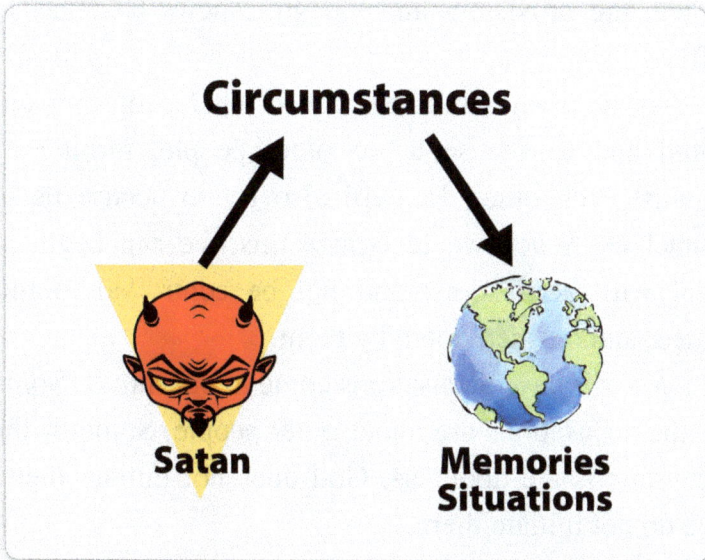

Image 2 -Circumstances Used to Manipulate Us

He presents facts that are true and then suggests the meaning behind them. He tells us what they mean in terms of value and purpose, life and future for us. He can never tell the truth. He's a liar.

In each situation, other people are involved in some way. Our experiences are connected to them and the situation. Because of that, we may associate the accusations and experiences with the people involved. The enemy stays hidden and brings accusations, telling us that they are the ones behind the accusations and judgments.

Satan will do all he can to deceive and accuse. This is how he functions. He is constantly against the truth, against us, and against our freedom. He is against the grace, the provision, and the good news God has to offer.

So, he always tries to accuse other people to our mind and to accuse us to other people, turning us against each other. He will also try to accuse us to ourselves. When we recognize this, we can begin to deal with accusations and not be controlled, dominated, and crushed down by them.

We will have accusations come to our minds. Some of the accusations are about other people. Some of the accusations are about us. God does not initiate them. We do not initiate them.

It is Satan who accuses.

- He is the author of all accusations and deceptions.
- He is the accuser of the brethren.
- He accuses us before God.
- He accuses us to ourselves.

How will Satan accuse? He will arrange circumstances in our life to occur and then bring his interpretation to it. People are usually involved in these situations. Satan will do all he can to deceive and accuse others to us and us to others.

What do we do with accusations?

- We learn to receive forgiveness.
- We learn to release.
- We grant forgiveness and release to others.

Let's say we have just gone through the process of forgiveness. We have released them (those we have forgiven) to the Lord. We have cancelled the debt they owe us. We have removed the *cork of unforgiveness*. We are now open and able to receive God's grace.

But let's say three or four days later, the person that we have forgiven does something again. All of the memories of what they did in the past that we forgave come back. What we found out is that Satan, who is the illegal god of this world, can use the experiences in the world and its situations to bring back our memories.

The accuser/prosecutor is not going to give up!
Read 1 John 5:4-12

We need to recognize when this happens. It's not God accusing us. We are not bringing the accusations back ourselves, because in order for us to do that we have to consciously say, "Now I'm going to remember what that person did and think about it."

Memories will be stirred up and used by the accuser.

The part of our soul which is our mind, has three parts to it.

There is the *conscious mind*, which is everything that we are aware of. Everything that we can recall, including the area of our emotions, feelings, and our will, only forms 10% of our mind.

The *unconscious mind* is like the memory banks, where information is stored, they are in the computer. The computer is on, but you don't see the information. Everything that has ever happened to us in life is recorded and it is in our subconscious and unconscious mind. You may not consciously be aware of it, but it's all there in our memory.

Let's take a look at this diagram.

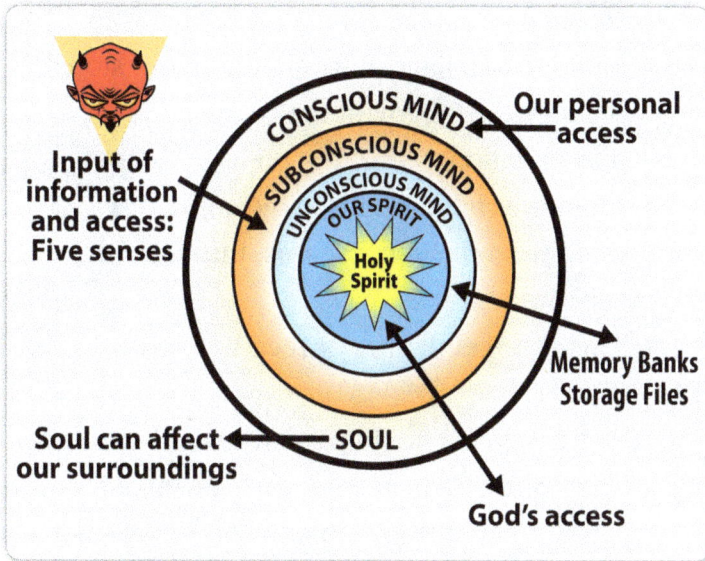

Image 3 -The Function of the Mind Within the Soul

Through our five senses, you and I receive input from the world around us. When that input comes in, it goes down and is added to the unconscious area of the mind. Nothing has been lost. This means that under the right conditions, we could bring something out of our *unconscious mind* and bring it to our *conscious mind*. We call that recall or memory.

Memories are stored in the unconscious mind.

- God has access to our mind by the Holy Spirit through our spirit.
- Satan attempts access through our five senses.
- Satan manipulates information in our stored memories, along with the negative interpretations.
- Memories are brought to the conscious mind from the unconscious, through the subconscious.
- This is remembering or recall.

Let's just say we could actually recall the experience of our birth. It is recorded. It is in our unconscious. This has been done. We may not be consciously aware of it, but we experienced it. Through our senses, the experience went in and was stored in our unconscious. This means every experience we have ever had is recorded. We may not be able to recall it, but it can be accessed and replayed. Sometimes it doesn't replay everything in our conscious mind. It replays the emotions we had. It replays some of the things we heard, or some of the tastes that we had at that time, or some of the smells, or the way things felt as we touched them.

Satan, being the illegal god of this world, was present when we experienced all of these things. So, he knows exactly what's been recorded. He knows how to get them to replay. He knows which password, or trigger, to use. He knows what part of the program he wants to replay. When memories were first being recorded and stored, Satan added negative meaning and interpretation to them. Along with this false interpretation, he will trigger the memory to replay in our subconscious and conscious mind.

> *In Revelation 12:9-10, we find out that*
> *Satan was the one who was kicked*
> *out of heaven. He deceives the*
> *whole world. It says in the last part*
> *of verse 10, "...for the accuser of*
> *the brethren has been thrown down,*
> *he who accuses them before our*
> *God day and night."*

He's identified as the; *accuser of the brethren,* and he accuses us before God, day and night. Have you experienced this? Most of the time we are deceived, and we think it is our self, someone else, or God accusing us. We have the Holy Spirit dwelling inside of us and He is able to access all of the memory banks within our spirit. We can also access those memory banks.

**But remember, there are three ways
our memories can be accessed.
It's either through God, or Satan, or us.**

When we have gone through the process to grant forgiveness, we have then released that person and ourself before God. This means we have torn up the debt they owe us and have given it to God. We say, "God, You have covered it with the blood of Jesus."

Then, are we going to purposefully say, "Now I want to remember what they did?" No, we're not going to do that. So, what happens when it comes to our mind? We should know it is not us. That just leaves two possibilities, God or Satan.

Usually, these accusations come to our mind when our mind is already consciously busy. We could be praying. We could be reading the scripture. We could be worshipping God. We could be concentrating on our work. We could be taking care of children. We could be washing the clothes. We could be talking to someone. When suddenly, a thought will occur. Maybe a mental picture begins to replay. We start physically feeling what we did in this memory and think, "Oh no, I'm doing it again!"

Then Satan says, "I thought you forgave them. You must not be a very good Christian. It's not God's fault, it must be you. There is something really wrong with you. Everyone else is okay, it's just you."

And then, we say, "I guess it is just me. Maybe I

can't be a good Christian! It must work for everyone else. I know God is okay, but I must be really bad."

This cycle can happen. Not only does Satan bring accusations against the other person, but then he accuses and condemns us for the memory of it being there, and he gets us to agree with him.

Image 4 -Satan Can Bring Accusing Thoughts To Mind

Who can access files in our memory?

God can

- Interject new thoughts or information
- Bring things to our mind

We can

- Recall information with thought assimilation and meditative process
- Come up with new or different thoughts or concepts

Satan

- Is involved in the programming and input
- Knows the password
- Can bring things to our conscious mind
- Can interject (suggest) new thoughts and ideas to our mind

Who brings up the offense we have forgiven?

Satan will. He is the tempter and the accuser. Remember, we just talked about how sins can come to your mind and we're shocked, but we should not be surprised. God is not going to bring that up. It's placed under the blood of Jesus. God says, *"I will remember those sins no more."*

You need to understand this. God is all-knowing. If God knows everything, how can He forget something? But God does not forget, He chooses not to bring it up from His memory. It's covered under the blood of Jesus. He chooses to leave it there. He says we can do the same.

But Satan will always bring those things to our mind. That's his job. We shouldn't be surprised when they come. We just need to know who it is. Satan is accusing us and he is tempting us.

We can learn to deal with the temptation and accusations.

Remember, the sin can be what others have done and it can be what we have done. Satan uses both.

Image 5 -Two Things Satan Uses to Accuse Us

How do we deal with accusations once they are forgiven?

Do we know how we have tried to deal with this in our life? We try to ignore it; pretend like it isn't there. Sometimes we try to fight with it.

We say, "No, leave! I'm not going to think about that." And then we think about it. The more we fight with it, the bigger it seems to get. Sometimes we say, "I'm just going to think happy thoughts." We try to think, "Oh, I'm so glad about this and this," because we're consciously trying to think about other things.

But the accusing thought is still in our subconscious. After a little time, we run out of happy thoughts. And there it is; it's still there! Sometimes we say, "I will just get really busy." So, we get really busy doing things, but eventually, we stop doing those things, and there it is. It's still there.

Past Sins Come To Mind:

- What others have done to us
- What we have done to others

Our Response Should Not Be:

- To ignore them
- To fight with them
- To try to think happy thoughts
- To try to cover them up with activity

Jesus is our Advocate: Hebrews 4:14-16.

Jesus, our Advocate, is also our High Priest, who is able to sympathize with our weaknesses and understands our temptations. He gives us access to the throne of grace, also known as the court room, so that we can receive mercy and grace in this time of need. It is where we can come with confidence to deal with the temptation and the accusation.

CHAPTER 4
STEPS TO DEALING WITH ACCUSATIONS

$\mathcal{S}$**tep One:**

- Admit it and agree that it happened.
- Do not waste energy and power: emotionally or mentally
- *James 1:2-4, Matthew 5:25*

Image 6 -Step One

What do we do when accusations bombard us?

First, we need to admit that it happened!

In James 1:2-4, there are three interesting verses.

> *In verse 2 it says, "Consider it all joy*
> *my brethren when you encounter*
> *various temptations."*

This is a temptation, but am I to consider this joy? In order to do this, I have to consciously interact with these verses.

> *In verse 3, "Knowing that the testing of*
> *your faith produces endurance."*

That is God's desired outcome for us. But, Satan wants to steal from us. God says, "I'm going to use it for you. You do what I say, and you will receive endurance."

> *Verse 4 says, "And let endurance have*
> *its perfect result, so that you may be*
> *perfect and complete, lacking in*
> *nothing."*

When that accusing thought comes, just say, "That's right. That occurred." Because it did, whether it was something someone did to us or what we did to them. That way we are not using all of our energy emotionally and mentally.

What Satan is always trying to do is to get us to expend the energy of our life where it won't have any benefit. When we habitually do this, we become depressed. If we overwork physically, we become fatigued and exhausted. If we overwork mentally and emotionally, where there's no real benefit, we are overwhelmed. When that occurs, the lies that Satan tells us sound true and we accept them. In this way, Satan is able to steal from us.

Image 7 -Step Two

Step Two:

- Interact with Jesus

- Superimpose the cross over this past sin
- Say: "Jesus, You died for this. It put You to death on the cross and Your blood was given to cover this."
- *Hebrews 9:11-14, 23-28; 10:9-25*

Use this opportunity to interact with Jesus.

See the cross over the sin that Satan is bringing up and accusing you to your mind.

You say, "Jesus, this put You to death on the cross. You died for this very purpose. Thank you Jesus, it was paid for in full."

It may be helpful if you write the accusing thoughts down so you can look at them and get them out of your mind so that you can deal with them with the Lord.

Image 8 -Step Three

Step Three:

- Go to the Father God
- Nail sins to the cross
- See the debt paid

Go to God, the Judge, and say, "Father God, You accepted Jesus' death as payment for these very sins. My sins have been paid for in full and the debt is cancelled. It is all under the blood of Jesus. It's been nailed to the cross."

Let me give you several scriptures to read:

- *2 Corinthians 5:15, 21*
- *Colossians 1:12-14, 19, 22*
- *Colossians 2:13-15*

**We continue our testimony or,
as it is also called, our confession of faith.**

This is all based upon what the scripture declares Jesus did with His body and blood, through the cross and resurrection. We are accepting the Judge's verdict and declaring that is the truth from which we live our life.

Step four
• **I am released**
• **I release others**

Image 9 -Step Four

Step Four:

- Declare - Say aloud, "I have been released and I have released others. I have been forgiven. I have been accepted by the Father. I have also forgiven others and I have released them. That is all under the blood of Jesus. All debts have been paid in full. All accusations have been cancelled by the Blood of Jesus, and the prison doors are opened. I and others are no longer imprisoned in my mind.
- *Ephesians 1:17-2:22* - You can expand your declarations and make them more

specific for your life based on these
scriptural truths.

As we have been considering these steps, don't just say
them in a repetitious way; make sure, as the diagrams
suggest, that you visualize these steps happening and
allow the Holy Spirit to renew you in the spirit of your
mind (*Ephesians 4:20-24*).

The Holy Spirit is the Spirit of Truth and the
Comforter, who was given to us to lead us into the
Truth and to apply God's grace and life to us. Based on
the divine exchange that Jesus accomplished on the
cross, He will give us life in place of death. The divine
life that we receive from God brings freedom, and joy
to live our lives to their full potential.

**In the first four steps,
you are submitting all of this to God.**

Satan brought it to your memory, but you are taking it,
and submitting it to God.

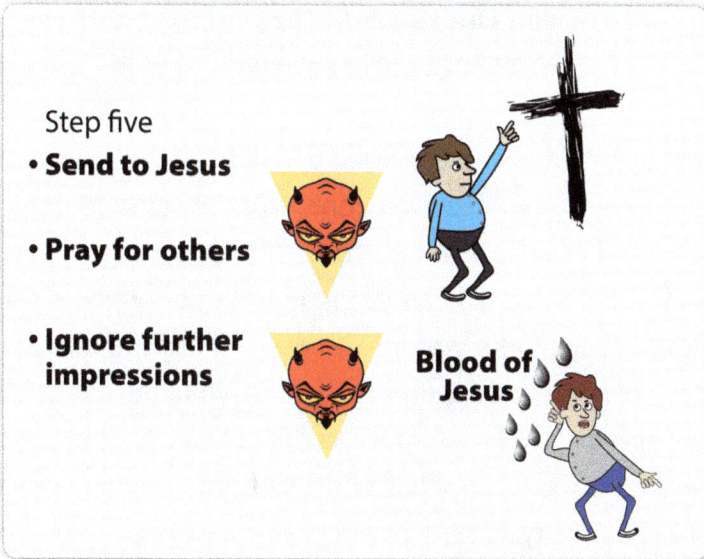

Image 10 - Step Five

Step Five:

- Say: "Satan, that is you, liar. If you want to argue with someone, go talk to my boss, Jesus." *James 4:7*
- After sending Satan to Jesus, pray for others. *Philippians 1:3-6, 9-11*
- Spend time praising the Lord and praying in the Spirit. *Philippians 4:4-8; Ephesians 5:19-20; Jude 1:20*
- Ignore any further impressions from Satan.

Now you can speak to the real problem
(Satan, the accuser).

You say, "Satan, that's you; you liar! If you want to fight and argue with someone, you go talk to Jesus. He's my boss. He's in charge of this, talk to Him."

Have you ever been doing a job and someone else comes by and tells you how to do it? They are not your boss. They are not even involved in your business, but they think they know more about it than anyone else. They try to tell you what to do. But you can tell them, "Go talk to my boss. I'm not going to talk to you; I'm busy." Well, that's what we need to do when Satan comes with all of these accusations and half-truths, also known as lies.

After you send Satan to Jesus, what do you do? You pray for others. Do you know why? Because by doing so, you focus your conscious mind on someone else. You are practicing splashing love on each other. It's more blessed to give. When you pray for someone else, you are asking God to pour His grace through you to others. God answers the prayer and the Holy Spirit begins pouring grace out upon that person.

Satan responds, "Oh, no. I've got to send troops over and try to counteract that." And God just pours out more grace.

A lot of that grace is coming through us. God has an endless supply of grace. The more we soak up, the more He gives out. When you finish praying everything you can pray for the person, you start rejoicing and praising the Lord, and praying in the Spirit. Then, if there are any little impressions from the enemy, you ignore them.

Have you ever laid in the sand or snow when you were a child? While you are lying there, you begin to move your legs and arms. When you get up, it looks like you made an angel. The other children watched you do this. You get up and they look at that impression. They go and look, but you're not there. It's just the impression of where you were.

When Satan brings an accusation to your mind, and you go through these five steps, you send Satan to Jesus, who is at the right-hand of the Father. He has to go. When he goes, he takes his accusation with him to accuse you in court before the Father. But there's an impression where it was in your mind. Do not try to interact with it, because nothing is there, just the impression. If you leave it alone, the wind of the Spirit will blow it away.

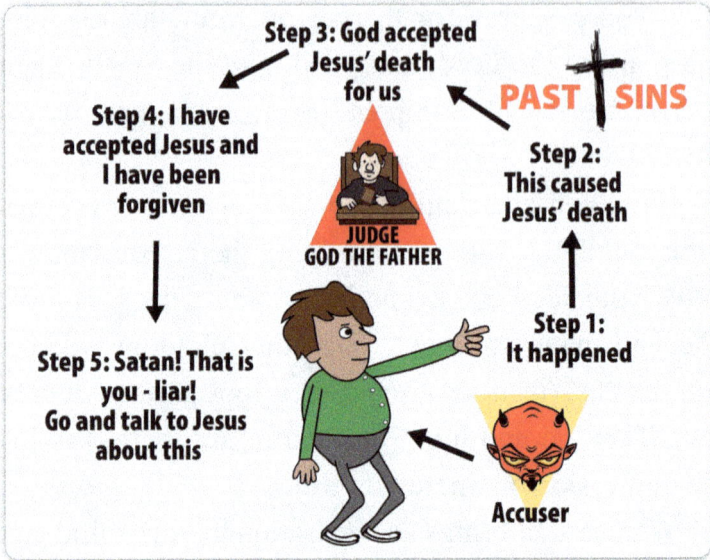

Image 11 - The Summary of All Five Steps

To Summarize:

Satan brings accusations to your mind. You agree that it happened. Then you begin to say, "Jesus died for this very thing. God, the Father, accepted Jesus' death and I've accepted Jesus and I've been forgiven. I've forgiven and released others. Satan, you are a liar. Go talk to Jesus about this." Then he has to appear in court.

CHAPTER 5
WHY WE NEED AN
ADVOCATE

*W*e need an advocate because the prosecutor is presenting his case and has access through sin and the law. Jesus' death met the requirements of the law and sin.

God, the Father, is the judge.
Where is He? He is in heaven.

Revelations 12:7-11 says that Satan will accuse us before God. We send him to God with his accusations. When we use Jesus' Name, we are exercising His authority and power, and Satan has no alternative but to appear in court. He takes his accusations with him to present his evidence as the prosecutor.

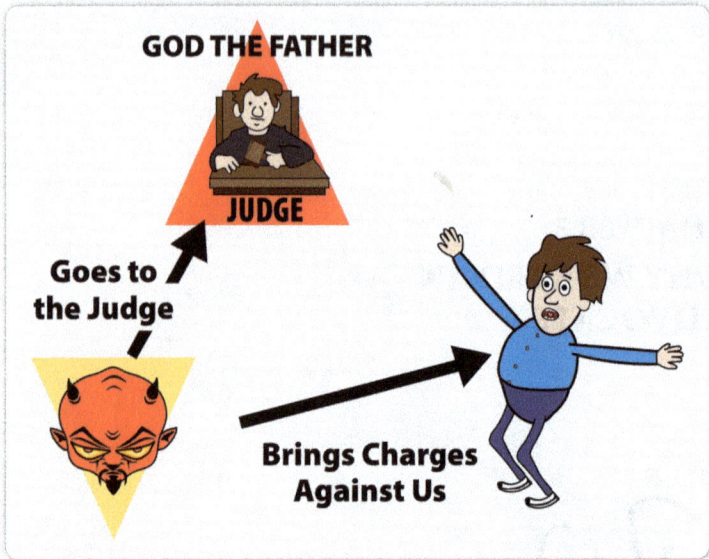

Image 12 -Satan Brings Charges Against Us

Here Satan appears. He brings the charges against you and presents them in court.

In the book of Job, he did the very same thing to Job (*Job 1:6-9*). Satan is the accuser, but he is also the prosecuting attorney. He's giving his presentation according to the law.

After his presentation, the Father says, "Who speaks for the defendant?" He asks, "Who speaks for this man?"

Jesus answers and says, "I do."

Jesus the advocate speaks for the Defendant

Image 13 - Jesus Speaks as Our Advocate

Remember, we have an advocate with the Father, who is seated at the right hand of God. He is ever interceding for us, on our behalf.

Jesus says, "I speak for him. He's accepted Me as his defense attorney, as his advocate. I will present his case. These charges have been paid for in full. Here's My blood. See my wounds and my stripes. Through these, he has been redeemed." (*I John 2:1-2; Hebrews 10:23-28; I Peter 2:24*)

Guess what?
Here Jesus has presented our case.

Do you know what the judge says?

He says, "I would like to hear the testimony of the defendant." He asks, "How do you plea?"

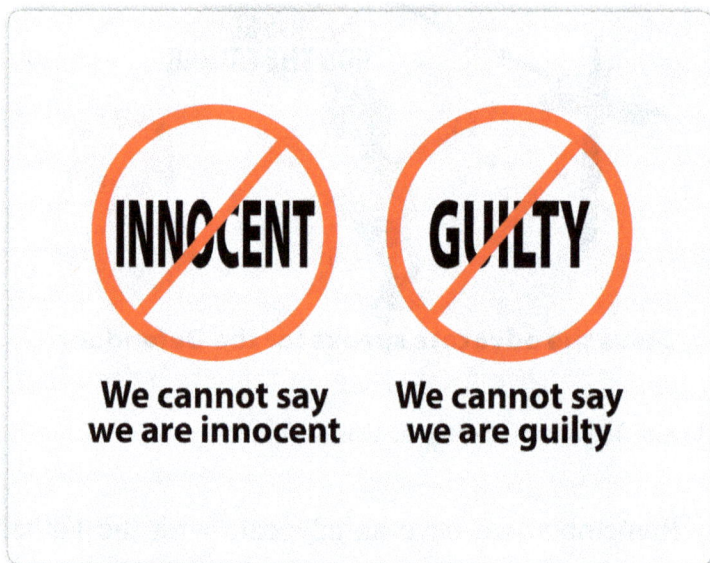

Image 14 -We Are Not Innocent or Guilty

We cannot say we are innocent. We cannot say we are guilty or we agree with the prosecutor. So how do we plea?

The Blood of Jesus, that's how we plea.

Revelation 12:10 says that Satan accuses us before God, day and night.

In verse 11, it says, "And they overcame

him because of the blood of the
Lamb and because of the word of
their testimony and they did not love
their life even when faced with
death."

We say, "My plea is the *blood of Jesus."*

We say, "Through the *blood of Jesus*, I've been redeemed. Through the *blood of Jesus*, I've been forgiven. Through the *blood of Jesus*, I am justified before God. Through the *blood of Jesus*, I am being sanctified, made holy, and set apart for God's purpose. My body is not my own; it's the temple for the Holy Spirit, bought and paid for through the *blood of Jesus*. Satan, you don't have any power in me. You have no power over me. My life is not my own, it belongs to Jesus. He is my Lord."

Image 15 -What is Our Plea?

Our witness stand, where we are giving testimony, is right here on earth. Remember, that is why Satan was accusing us through our own mind. Now he is in court before God, where we sent him, where he's accusing us. Jesus is there as our attorney, presenting His case on our behalf. The Father says, "I want to hear your testimony."

Jesus says, "I won't leave you alone. I will give you another counselor (attorney), the Holy Spirit, who will be with you. He will tell you what to say, at the time you will need it."

Image 16 -Agree with Jesus & Plea the Blood

The enemy is trying to get us to agree with him. The Holy Spirit is saying, "Don't believe it; it's a lie." The enemy yells at us. He says, "You are wrong. You do all these bad things. You don't deserve God.

The Holy Spirit says, "Don't believe him. He's a liar. It is written, Jesus died for you. You are not condemned. You are forgiven. You are born again and you are a new creation." The still small voice of the Holy Spirit does not yell. We need to listen to Him. He is the Spirit of Truth.

If we agree with our accuser, what does that do to our attorney's case?

- If we accept the accusations, Jesus will say, "Oh Father, he doesn't know what he is saying. He is deceived, don't listen to him."

- And the Holy Spirit is saying to us, "It's not true, these accusations are not true. Because Jesus' Blood has already taken care of it. It is written in the scripture."

Jesus is the Truth and He is the Way, and He is the Life. Nobody goes to the Father, except through Him. That is how we go to the Father. Whatever He says about us is the truth. It is the truth because He is Truth! It doesn't matter what anyone else says, it will all be a lie compared to what He says. When we agree with Him, we experience victory. He makes us to be more than conquerors in Christ Jesus.

Image 17 -Not Guilty

We have agreed with our attorney. We have made our testimony based on the *blood of Jesus*. The *blood of Jesus* is between us and the lies and accusations.

The Father says, "Not guilty. Case dismissed."

> *In Matthew 12:37, there is an important verse. "For by your words you will be justified and by your words you will be condemned."*

It is our word of testimony about what God's Word says; what the *blood of Jesus* does for us.

God the Father says, "You are not guilty; case

dismissed. Be it done unto you according to your word."

What if we continue to agree with our accuser?

- When we agree with our accuser, that becomes our testimony.
- Scripture says that at the word of two witnesses, something will be established. God looks and he knows it's been paid for, but we're agreeing with our accuser. He is obligated to say, "Be it done according to your words."
- Then, the Holy Spirit will continue to say to us, "You need to change your testimony to agree with Jesus, your attorney."
- We would need to retake this to court and change the testimony.

Do you see how important this is? Because Satan's job is to accuse you to yourself, to accuse you to other people, and to accuse other people to you. This is also called temptation.

So, when we go to God and deal with it, we're set free! We walk in freedom. God loves you. He pours out His grace upon you. He says, "I am never accusing you. I give you life. Come and receive it! I give you life."

MORE TOPICS IN THIS SERIES

Titles in this series: 13

The first six booklets in this series are centered on repairing, restoring, healing, and transforming areas of our past.

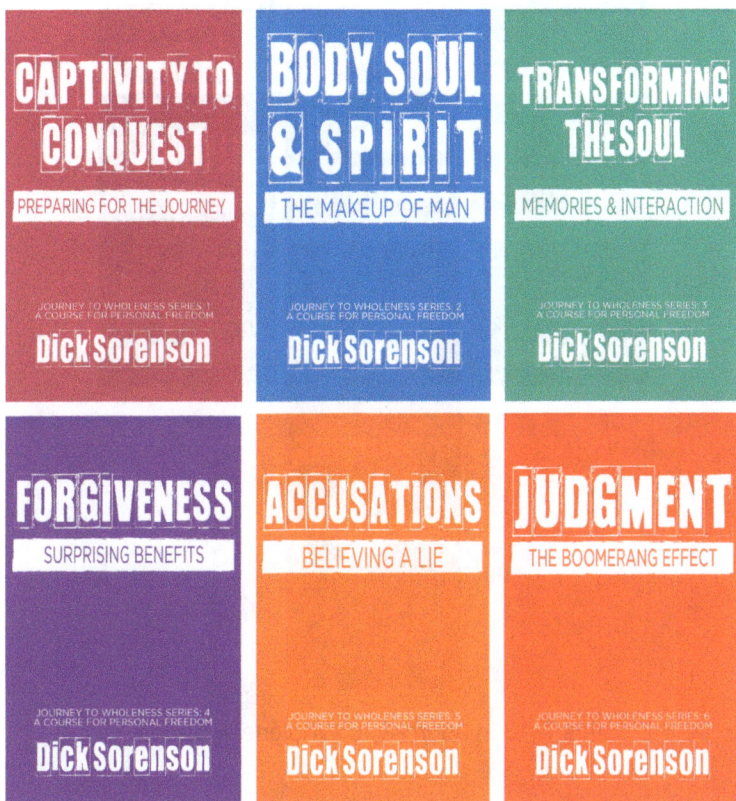

CAPTIVITY TO CONQUEST
PREPARING FOR THE JOURNEY
JOURNEY TO WHOLENESS SERIES 1
A COURSE FOR PERSONAL FREEDOM
Dick Sorenson

BODY SOUL & SPIRIT
THE MAKEUP OF MAN
JOURNEY TO WHOLENESS SERIES 2
A COURSE FOR PERSONAL FREEDOM
Dick Sorenson

TRANSFORMING THE SOUL
MEMORIES & INTERACTION
JOURNEY TO WHOLENESS SERIES 3
A COURSE FOR PERSONAL FREEDOM
Dick Sorenson

FORGIVENESS
SURPRISING BENEFITS
JOURNEY TO WHOLENESS SERIES: 4
A COURSE FOR PERSONAL FREEDOM
Dick Sorenson

ACCUSATIONS
BELIEVING A LIE
JOURNEY TO WHOLENESS SERIES: 5
A COURSE FOR PERSONAL FREEDOM
Dick Sorenson

JUDGMENT
THE BOOMERANG EFFECT
JOURNEY TO WHOLENESS SERIES: 6
A COURSE FOR PERSONAL FREEDOM
Dick Sorenson

Titles 1-6 in Journey to Wholeness Series

As we move on through the next 7 booklets, we'll be breaking free and rebuilding, replacing lies with truth, standing against the attacks of the enemy, pulling down strongholds, and we will be setting free what is bound.

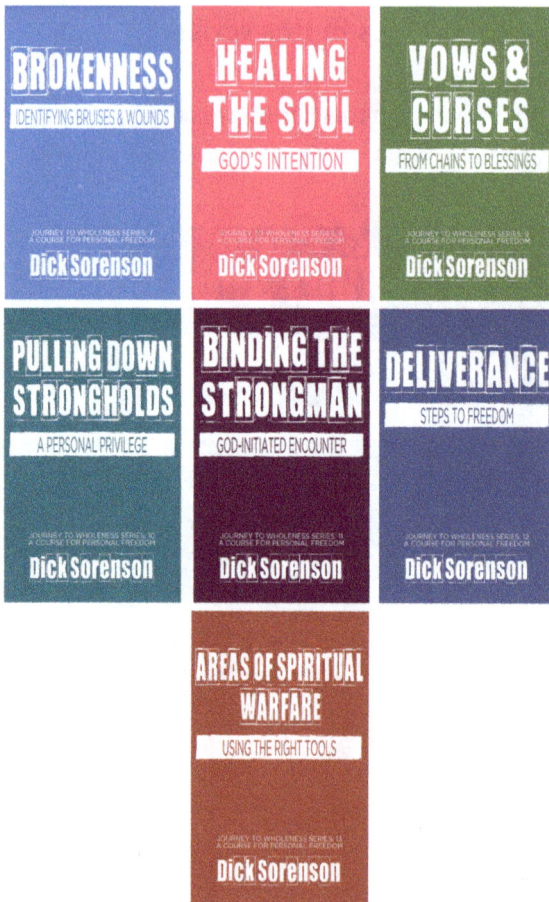

BROKENNESS
IDENTIFYING BRUISES & WOUNDS

JOURNEY TO WHOLENESS SERIES 7
A COURSE FOR PERSONAL FREEDOM
Dick Sorenson

HEALING THE SOUL
GOD'S INTENTION

JOURNEY TO WHOLENESS SERIES 8
A COURSE FOR PERSONAL FREEDOM
Dick Sorenson

VOWS & CURSES
FROM CHAINS TO BLESSINGS

JOURNEY TO WHOLENESS SERIES 9
A COURSE FOR PERSONAL FREEDOM
Dick Sorenson

PULLING DOWN STRONGHOLDS
A PERSONAL PRIVILEGE

JOURNEY TO WHOLENESS SERIES 10
A COURSE FOR PERSONAL FREEDOM
Dick Sorenson

BINDING THE STRONGMAN
GOD-INITIATED ENCOUNTER

JOURNEY TO WHOLENESS SERIES 11
A COURSE FOR PERSONAL FREEDOM
Dick Sorenson

DELIVERANCE
STEPS TO FREEDOM

JOURNEY TO WHOLENESS SERIES 12
A COURSE FOR PERSONAL FREEDOM
Dick Sorenson

AREAS OF SPIRITUAL WARFARE
USING THE RIGHT TOOLS

JOURNEY TO WHOLENESS SERIES 13
A COURSE FOR PERSONAL FREEDOM
Dick Sorenson

Titles 7-13 in Journey to Wholeness Series

That's good! It's not something we do just once; it's a lifestyle we learn to live with. Because of the rebellion, and the result of war Satan started in heaven, and brought to earth, you and I are in spiritual warfare. We will talk about spiritual warfare, look at the overview and then go over what is happening up close and personal in our lives.

Journey to Wholeness Series

1. Captivity to Conquest - *Preparing for the Journey*
2. Body, Soul & Spirit - *The Makeup of Man*
3. Transforming the Soul - *Memories & Interaction*
4. Forgiveness - *Surprising Benefits*
5. Accusations - *Believing a Lie*
6. Judgment - *The Boomerang Effect*
7. Brokenness - *Identifying Bruises and Wounds*
8. Healing of the Soul - *God's Intention*
9. Vows & Curses- *From Chains to Blessings*
10. Pulling Down Strongholds - *A Personal Privilege*
11. Binding the Strongman - *God Initiated Encounter*
12. Deliverance - *Steps to Freedom*
13. Areas of Spiritual Warfare - *Using the Right Tools*

About this Series

The *Journey to Wholeness* series is designed to be used as a guide or study to bring an individual into personal freedom and spiritual maturity. It is also designed to use as a study guide for a small gathering, home group, or a classroom setting. This material is a resource for leading a discipleship group, personal growth group, or teaching a series for ministry training. Each topic is a separate booklet. Although all topics fit together to become the *Journey to Wholeness*, each can be discovered and applied separately to impart life, freedom, and spiritual growth as needed.

The way this series became available is rather unique since every single word in these booklets was spoken. The contents of this series have been compiled from PowerPoint slides, the seminar workbook, and transcribed audio recordings on wholeness Dick delivered at a training center in Cairo, Egypt. This series is an original course of Dick Sorenson Ministries.

Thank you for your participation in this series.

Hiking toward hope on a personal journey to wholeness…

If you've gained insight, we invite you to share your thoughts with us. You can do this in several ways:

- Leave a review
- Share on social media using the hashtags #j2wSeries, #dicksorenson, #thelanyaplifebooks and tagging us @thelanyaplife
- Contact us through our website thelanyaplife.com

OTHER BOOKS

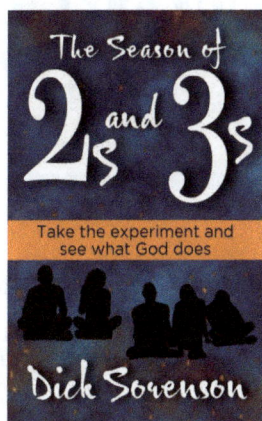

The Season of 2s & 3s: take the experiment and see what God does —by Dick Sorenson

We are called to be the Lord's ambassadors and to be more than conquerors in the dominion of darkness. This call will affect history and bring about God's purposes. But we do not do the work, God does, and

He will use the agreement of just 2 or 3 to bring it about.

Dick Sorenson gives a powerful account of an experience he had over 30 years ago and shares how God is bringing it all together with past and present visions to let us know the time is now.

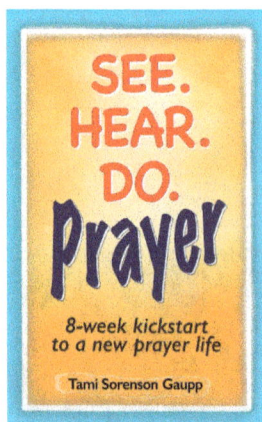

See. Hear. Do. Prayer: 8-week kickstart to a new prayer life— by Tami Sorenson Gaupp

Prayer doesn't look the same for everyone. Find out how to make your prayer life an adventure! In *See. Hear. Do. Prayer,* you'll be led to the heart of God, as Tami takes you on an adventure through this 8-week kickstart in prayer.

ww.thelanyaplife.com/books

ABOUT THE AUTHOR

Dick Sorenson was born in Twin Falls, Idaho, in 1946. When he was one day old, he was adopted into a loving non-Christian family and raised as an only child. At the age of three, his family moved to Nevada, where he grew up in the rough and tumble "wild west" environment for ten years before moving back to Idaho.

Dick experienced a life-changing encounter with Jesus Christ while reading the Gospels. He accepted Jesus as his Savior and was born again. A few weeks later, on Easter Sunday, he was baptized in water. It was also his fifteenth birthday. Two years later, he had another course-altering encounter that lead him to give up two college scholarships, one in nuclear physics and one in wrestling, to pursue full-time ministry. Then a scholarship was offered for him to attend Central Christian College of the Bible in Moberly, Missouri. He studied Hebrew for one year and studied Greek for three years. He furthered his education at Eastern New Mexico University, in Portales, New Mexico, receiving a double Master's Degree in Counseling and Theology.

At age 20, Dick planted two new churches while still in college.

Since giving his life to full-time ministry in 1966, God has worked through him in resolving church conflicts, helping churches understand Biblical leadership, imparting vision, and as a resource for pastors and missionaries. In 1974, he started one of the first Christian Counseling practices in the State of Idaho, which served the community for fifteen years. Traveling internationally since 1983, including ministry to unreached people groups, he has ministered in over one hundred countries, training leaders, and conducting seminars around the world. His non-denominational approach has reached across denominational lines, resulting in many lives touched through teaching, counseling, prayer, and deliverance ministry.

Dick has a heart for the Nations and the workers in the field, taking teams for work projects, teaching the Word, and prayer-walking in restricted access areas of the world. His passion is to prepare and urge people to step out in the call God has for them. He sits on three ministry boards and currently resides in Boise, Idaho, with his wife Donna, to whom he has been happily married to for over fifty-five years. They have two married children, two married grandsons, and two great-granddaughters.

Dick and Donna live to fellowship—
anywhere, anytime, and over coffee
preferably!

SPECIAL THANKS

Many thanks to all those who have prayed, contributed to, and encouraged us to complete this series. We could not have accomplished this without your help.

May God bless you on your journey!

Donna Sorenson...
You are the one who made it happen. Your love and vision prompted each of us to see the importance of transferring "what was in Dick's head" to words on paper... You are the strength and spark.

Tami Gaupp...
Our daughter was an answer to our prayers for help. We value her encouragement and push – she took this project from a seminar format to a booklet series by her persistence in learning new things... setting up a publishing company, book design, and publishing.

Rick Sorenson…
Our son spent countless hours and days interacting with Dick, sorting out the life-application of each subject while applying them personally and giving feedback… always over a good cup of coffee.

Becky Hansen…
Her design skills have been an invaluable asset as she created and recreated diagrams and a cover… with laughter, sometimes tears, but always with patience for us.

Pam Pearson…
Who patiently spent day after day transcribing the recordings from Dick's teaching in Egypt the old-fashioned way… listen, stop, type, repeat.

Cindy Anderson…
Was part of the initial work to get us started, using her writing skills in outlining and putting a structure to this material.

Fount Shults…
Gave his time to Dick, studying and engaging in endless hours of fruitful discussion.

What a blessing you all are to us…